Let's Take a Trip

An Air Show Adventure

by Deborah Crisfield

photography by Donald Emmerich

Troll Associates

Library of Congress Cataloging-in-Publication Data

Crisfield, Deborah.
    An air show adventure / by Deborah Crisfield; photography by
Donald Emmerich.
        p.   cm.—(Let's take a trip)
    Summary: Describes events at the EAA Fly-in, an air show held in
Oshkosh, Wisconsin, focusing on the unique aircraft on display.
    ISBN 0-8167-1735-4 (lib. bdg.)   ISBN 0-8167-1736-2 (pbk.)
    1. Air shows—Wisconsin—Oshkosh—Juvenile literature. [1. Air
shows. 2. Airplanes.] I. Emmerich, Donald, ill. II. Title.
III. Series.
TL721.6.O84C75   1990
797.5—dc20   89-34372

The author and the publisher wish to thank John Burton, Richard Matt, Norman Petersen, and the Experimental
Aircraft Association for their generous assistance and cooperation, and to acknowledge the following for their
photographs: The Smithsonian Institute, p. 3; NASA, p. 16 (inset); Stoddard-Hamilton Aircraft, Inc., p. 24 (top);
John Levy, p. 24 (bottom); Norman Petersen, p. 26 (top); Keith Photography, p. 26 (bottom); and the EAA, p. 27, top
photos by Jim Koepnick, bottom photo by Don Hedke.

People have always dreamed of soaring through the sky like the birds. Two brothers named Wilbur and Orville Wright had this dream, and in 1903 it finally came true. In an airplane they had built themselves, they made the first successful powered flight. Since then, thousands of people have built their own airplanes or restored old ones.

Each year thousands of these airplane owners gather at a special event, the EAA Fly-In Convention. Let's join Laura and Stevie Reese and their parents for a week-long adventure that includes exciting air shows. Before taking off, Mr. Reese carefully checks his airplane to be sure that everything is working properly.

As they fly over the airfield at Oshkosh, Wisconsin, the Reeses see that many airplanes have already arrived. The air-traffic controllers in the tower are in charge of directing the air traffic—the 15,000 aircraft that come and go throughout the week of the Fly-In. With 64,000 take-offs and landings during that week, the airport is four times busier than some of the largest airports in the world.

The Reeses park their airplane in an area reserved for aircraft that were built in the 1940s and 50s. A flight-line-crew volunteer helps them find a spot. Some people have pitched tents right next to their airplanes, but Laura and Stevie are glad that theirs is in a grove of trees, where it will be cooler. The children are eager to go see a big blimp that is flying low nearby and is about to land.

The blimp has two engines, which move it through the air at about 35 miles an hour. To make the airship go up and down, the pilot has to push hard on the foot pedals. When the blimp is almost down, members of the ground crew grab a long cable that is dangling from its nose and attach it to a tall mast. The blimp is filled with helium, just like party balloons, and it would float away if it were not tied down.

A special thrill for people at the Fly-In is seeing the Concorde, a supersonic airplane. Unlike the fat, slow blimp, the sleek Concorde has four big Rolls Royce engines and flies at 1,550 miles an hour. That is more than twice the speed of sound! When it takes off and lands, the noise is tremendous.

The Concorde is one of the fastest commercial airliners in the world. It can carry 100 passengers from London, England, to New York City in less than three hours. Other flights between these two cities usually take from six to eight hours. Some lucky people at the Fly-In even take a ninety-minute ride in this special airplane.

A crowd has also gathered for a demonstration of the U.S. Marine Corps Harrier jets. The Harrier jets are unusual because, like a helicopter, they can take off and land vertically, or straight up and down, and also turn and move sideways. This allows them to take off and land on a short runway. Notice how the hot exhaust under the Harrier makes the trees and buildings in the background look distorted.

Later, Laura and Stevie stop to talk to the Eagle, the official EAA Fly-In mascot. He suggests that the children look at the antique airplanes. They arrive just in time to see a man take off in a Curtis Pusher, a copy of an airplane that was flown in 1911. The pilot's clothes—knickers, boots and goggles—are similar to what the pilots wore in the early days of flying.

Old airplanes with two pairs of wings, one on top of the other, are called biplanes. Laura and Stevie sit in one that was flown to Wisconsin all the way from Florida. Flying at about 50 miles an hour, the trip took five days. The owner spent three years building the biplane, using parts from a great number of old airplanes.

Nearby are many other kinds of old airplanes.
There are rows and rows of colorful Beechcraft—
airplanes that were popular in the 1930s.
Gyroplanes, which are similar to helicopters, were
invented in the early 1920s. During take-off, a
motor spins the rotor blades on top of the
gyroplane. But during flight, the motor just turns
a small propeller to give the gyroplane forward
motion. The rotor blades continue to spin because
of air pressure against them.

Each year over eight hundred thousand men, women, and children attend the Fly-In. It takes a lot of planning to take care of so many people during a one-week period. Over four hundred thousand sodas are sold to thirsty people, and five thousand blocks of ice are used to keep the drinks cold. The campgrounds next to the airfield are filled with forty thousand campers.

Not everyone who visits the Fly-In owns an airplane or is even a pilot. People come from all over the United States and as far away as Japan just to see the thousands of different airplanes and be part of all the activities. Some take part in a Parade of Nations, proudly carrying the flags of their countries.

Sometimes there are speeches by people who have had an important role in aviation history. Neil Armstrong, the first man to land and walk on the surface of the moon, has flown more than two hundred different models of aircraft. These include jets, rockets, helicopters, and gliders.

For many people, including Laura and Stevie, the most exciting event is the air show. Everyone's eyes are glued to the sky as the air show begins. Suddenly the crowd notices that parachutists have jumped from several airplanes that just flew over, far above the runway. Soon they can see the Liberty Parachute team floating down, trailing colorful flags from many countries.

Some of the most highly trained pilots in the world perform at the air show. A big attraction is the Warbirds, restored airplanes that flew in World War II. Squadrons of these historic airplanes fly in formation, leaving trails of smoke behind them. The Japanese airplanes are easy to spot with the rising red sun painted on their sides.

The air show also features some of the world's best aerobatic teams. Aerobatics are acrobatic tricks in the air. Twisting and turning, these pilots skillfully weave their red, white and blue airplanes in and out of each other's paths. The crowd watches in awe as two airplanes make a close pass just above the runway.

The three pilots of the Eagles Aerobatic Team move together in perfect harmony. They start their aerial dance by streaking through the sky in formation and then suddenly splitting and flying off in three different directions. Two of the airplanes come together again, but this time one is flying upside down right over the other!

One of the favorite parts of the show is a dare-devil trick—someone rides on a special platform attached to the upper wing while the pilot performs aerobatic stunts. The scariest part for the rider must be when the airplane is flying upside down. At the end of the air show all the pilots ride by in jeeps, waving to the crowd.

After the show, youngsters can take part in a workshop in one of the big tents. Experienced teenagers teach youngsters how to build their own model airplane wings. A young visitor from England proudly inspects the wing he has built.

Students at a local high school are building an airplane through a program known as Project Schoolflight. The students' partly-finished airplane is on display at the Fly-In. Many students who are active in the Project Schoolflight program later go into careers in aviation.

Approximately two thousand of the aircraft at the Fly-In are home-built. Many people who build their own airplanes use a kit that contains most of the necessary parts—the engine always has to be purchased separately. Even when friends are working together, it takes hundreds of hours to assemble a kit airplane like this Glasair.

A Glasair is a modern, high performance airplane made from fiber glass. The owner tells Stevie that the airplane can fly across the country at speeds from 250 to 290 miles an hour. It also can do aerobatics. Flying the Glasair is similar to flying a jet fighter.

Rather than use a kit, some people build their airplanes from scratch. *Blueprints*, or detailed drawings of the aircraft, show and describe each piece of the airplane. It took six years to build the "Starduster Too." Every part was handmade except for the engine, propeller, and wheels.

One of the most famous airplanes to be built by individuals is the Voyager. The unique design of this airplane enabled its pilots, Dick Rutan and Jeana Yeager, to set a distance record by flying around the world non-stop. They didn't have to land during the entire trip to get more fuel. After visiting the Fly-In, the Voyager was taken to the Smithsonian's Air and Space Museum in Washington, D.C.

While at the Fly-In, visitors often tour the EAA Air Adventure Museum to learn more about the history of aviation. The Museum houses the largest private aircraft collection in the world, as well as *replicas*, or copies, of some well-known historical aircraft, such as the one built by the Wright Brothers. This detailed replica of the Wright Brothers' airplane shows how Orville lay on the wings of the airplane during the first flight.

Another popular replica at the Museum is the Spirit of St. Louis. In 1927 Charles A. Lindbergh flew the original Spirit of St. Louis from New York to Paris. It was the first time anyone had flown solo across the Atlantic Ocean. Mr. Lindbergh had five sandwiches with him for the flight, which lasted thirty-three and a half hours, but he only had time to finish one.

This may look like a toy, but it's really the world's smallest twin-engine airplane. Named the Cricket by its French designer, it was not flown in the United States until 1981. Another interesting airplane on display in the Air Museum is the BD-5, the type of aerobatic airplane that was used in a James Bond movie. It can fly faster than 200 miles an hour.

People first flew in the sky in balloons and gliders, like this replica of the Chanute hang glider of 1896. The Wright brothers and others before them learned valuable information about *aerodynamic lift*, or the force of air in motion, by making hundreds of glider flights. Some gliders today can reach speeds of over 100 miles an hour and stay in the air for hours, all without power.

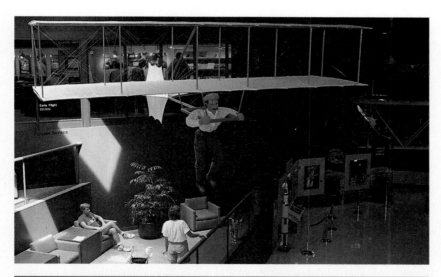

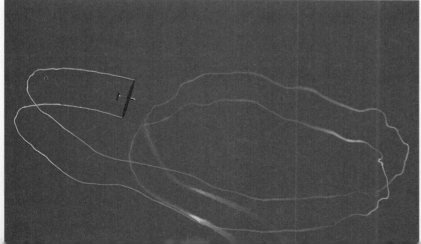

Many major advances in aviation technology have been achieved by ordinary people building their own aircraft in garages like this. The sign on the garage says that people "....have in the past and will in the future build their own wings on dreams." What new types of aircraft will be created in the twenty-first century? What new dreams of flight do you think will become reality?